Collector's Digest
Dexterity Games
And Other Hand-Held Puzzles

© 1995
L-W Book Sales

ISBN#: 0-89538-029-3

Published by: L-W Book Sales
              P.O. Box 69
              Gas City, IN 46933

Photography by David Devon Dilley

Please write for our free catalog.

Attention Collectors . . . if you would like to contribute photographs or
information of your collection (possibly for profit), please call L-W Books
(toll free) at 1-800-777-6450 Tuesday thru Friday 9am to 3pm.

Special thanks are owed to Patt DeHaan for contributing information and photographs without which *Dexterity Games and Other Hand-Held Puzzles* would not
be possible. Dexterity game collectors and enthusiasts feel free to contact her at
the following number: *Antiques and Collectibles by Patt* 1 (616) 842-3460.

Preface

Dexterity games (also known as "pocket puzzles" or "hand-held" games) have entertained children and collectors throughout the last century. A fairly cheap alternative to the more expensive toys spurred massive popularity of these games during the years of the Depression, and retained its grip on the toy market through the years to follow. A young child could spend hours honing his hand-eye coordination (perhaps a distant precursor to the now contemporary "video game") before he could master his dexterity game, much to the envy of his "clumsier" playmates.

Dexterity puzzles (as examined in this volume) are typically small round or square puzzles with movable pieces enclosed within a cardboard or wooden frame and transparent glass or plastic window, thus all of the internal workings are clearly evident (in most cases). These games are then shaken, wiggled, nudged, or tilted in order to send the mobile playing piece to its proper destination point, often a slightly recessed cavity or partially enclosed "stall". The inside of the toy visible through the window usually had vibrant scenes printed upon it, thus offering a setting and instructions for the game.

Dexterity games have often been discovered in recent years past, hiding within collections or display showcases along with dozens of other trinkets, toys, tools, etc. Many collectors acquire hand-held games as a supplement to their usual collection, as advertising and character picture prints were quite popular among these game manufacturers. These games were included within many interests due to the variety of subjects they represented, such as outer space games, cowboys, black memorabilia, War-era propaganda, animals, and many others.

The prevalence of pocket puzzles throughout today's collector's market has inspired many toy collectors to concentrate on dexterity games alone. Once available in drugstores, dimestores, and lurking as prizes in the bottom of Cracker Jack boxes decades ago, now avid hunters are combing through boxes and showcases of small toys in order to discover their new find. Armed with perseverance, enthusiasm, and a copy of "*Dexterity Games and Other Hand-Held Puzzles*", their quarry can't elude them for too long.

Table Of Contents

PRICING NOTE

The following values listed herein have been determined from observed prices in antique shows, collector's malls, and antique dealer shops. The values are averaged from various sources (as noted above) and represent items in excellent condition.

Advertising Puzzles

Holsum Bread
Tin & Plastic
2 1/4" Dia.
$20

TastyKake
Kirchhof Advertising
1 1/4" Dia.
$15

Ring Around A Rosy Game
[Cook Oil Co. Advertisement]
Cardboard & Plastic
2 1/4" Dia.
$35

Keep Your Eyes on Herefords
Tin & Plastic
1 1/4" Dia.
$15

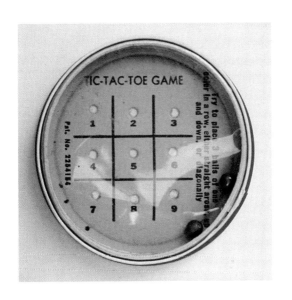

Tic-Tac-Toe Game
[1959 Air Control Picnic Advertisement]
Cardboard & Plastic
2 1/4" Dia.
$15

Humpty Dumpty
[Marshall Field & Co. Advertisement]
Cardboard & Plastic
2 1/4" Dia.
$25

Carstairs White Seal Whiskey
Cardboard & Plastic
2 3/4" Dia.
$25

Dog N' Suds
Tin & Plastic
1 1/4" Dia.
$12

Red Goose Shoes (Top & Bottom View)
Cardboard & Plastic
2 1/4" Dia.
$25

Tip-Top Bread (Top & Bottom View)
Cardboard, Plastic, & Rivets
2" x 2"   1951
$20

Panama Locks (Top & Bottom View)
Tin & Brass   1915
2" x 2"
$100

Elsie the Borden Cow (Borden Co.)
Tin, Glass, & Cardboard
2 1/2" x 3 1/2"   1941
$125

Cocoa Marsh
Tin & Plastic
1 1/4" Dia.
$30

Sailor Duck (The Shoe Box - Family Shoe Store, Brookfield, MO)
Plastic, Cardboard, & Foil
2 3/8" Dia.
$25

McDonalds Corp.
Tin & Plastic
1 1/4" Dia.   1964
$55

Quaker City Life Ins. Co.
[L. Gimbel]
Tin & Plastic
1 1/4" Dia.
$25

Clown Face (Muffets)
Tin & Plastic
1 1/4" Dia.
$25

Elephant (Muffets)
Tin & Plastic
1 1/4" Dia.
$25

Clown with Feet (Muffets)
Tin & Plastic
1 1/4" Dia.
$25

Tiger (Muffets)
Tin & Plastic
1 1/4" Dia.
$25

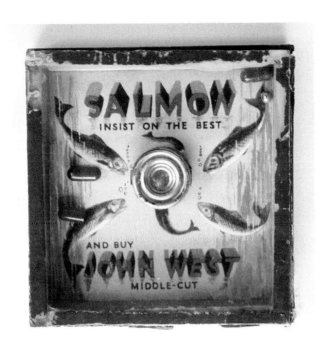

John West Salmon
Glass & Wood
3 1/4" x 3 1/4"
$60

International Tailoring Co.
Tin & Glass (Mirror on Back)
1 7/8" Dia.
$125

Royal National Life-Boat Institution
[Made in England]
Tin, Glass, & Cardboard
3" x 3"
$35

New Holland -(New Super
Hayliner 78)
Tin & Plastic
2 1/8" Dia.
$30

General Electric
Tin & Plastic
1 3/8" Dia.   ca. 1960s
$30

Woman in Spanish Garb
[General Electric]
1 1/4" Dia.   1960
$25

PM Blended Whiskey
Plastic & Cardboard
2 7/8" x 3/8"
$30

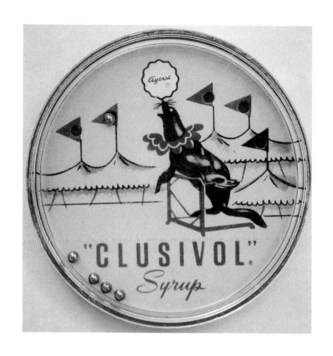

Ayerst "Clusivol" Syrup
[Wagner Plastic Corp.]
Plastic & Cardboard
3" Dia.
$25

Ask for Cherry Blossoms
[Made in Germany]
Aluminum, Glass, & Cardboard
1 3/8" Dia.
$50

"Clusivol" Syrup
[Wagner Plastic Corp.]
Plastic
3" Dia.
$30

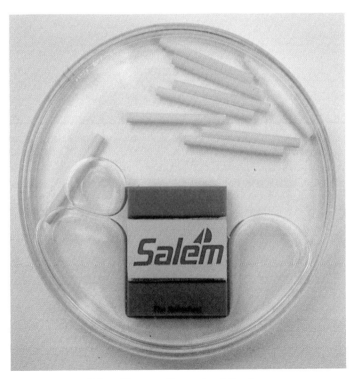

Salem Cigarettes Promotional Puzzle
Plastic (Filled with Fluid)
3 3/4" Dia.
$25

The "Tantalizer Puzzle"
[American Puzzle Co.]
Wood & Glass
2 5/8" x 2 1/8"
$60
(Advertising on side pictured below)

Eaton's Santa Claus in Toyland
(Reverse side shown below)
Aluminum, Glass & Cardboard
1 3/4" Dia.
$70

Texaco Fire-Chief (Reproduction)
[The Texas Co.]
Plastic & Cardboard
2 3/4" Dia.
$15

Sohio Gasoline
(Reproduction)
(Calendar on Back)
Plastic & Cardboard
2 3/4" Dia.
$15

Airplane Puzzles

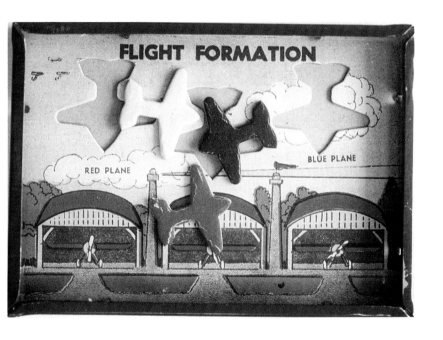

Flight Formation
Tin, Glass, & Cardboard
5" x 3 1/2"
$40

Graf Zeppelin Puzzle
[Made in Germany]
Plastic
2 1/4" Dia.
$15

Following Page (Upper Photo)
New York to Paris Aero Race
[Par-Zim Toy Mfg. Co., Inc.]
Tin, Glass, & Cardboard
4 1/8" x 3 1/2"
$85

Following Page (Lower Photo)
The Bomber
Tin & Glass
3 1/2" x 5"
$70

(Above) See Previous Page

(Below) See Previous Page

Global Airmail Puzzle
Glass & Paper
5" x 4"
$30

Jet Fighter Game (Pinball-Style)
Tin, Glass, Wood, & Cardboard
2 5/16" x 4 3/8"
$50

Black Memorabilia

Star Soap
Metal & Glass (with Mirror on Back)
2" Dia.
$110

Natives & Alligators
[Made in Occupied Japan]
Glass, Aluminum, & Cardboard (with Mirror on Back)
2 1/4" Dia.
$50

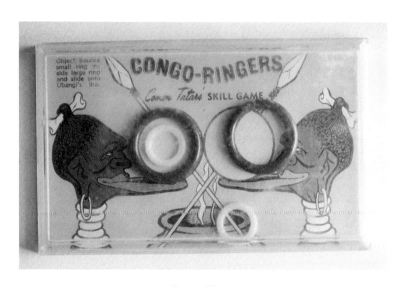

Congo-Ringers
Plastic
5" x 3"
$35

Black Man Puffing Smoke
[Made in Germany]
Metal & Glass
1 3/4" Dia.
$80

(Above) Black Man with Red Tie & Hat
Metal, Glass, & Cardboard
(with Mirror on Back)
2 1/4" Dia.
$90

(Below) Native on Ostrich
Metal & Glass (with Mirror on Back)
2 1/4" Dia.
$75

Cartoon Character Puzzles

Popeye the Juggler
(King Features Syndicate)
[Bar Zim Toy Mfg. Co.]
Tin & Glass
3 1/2" x 5"
$70

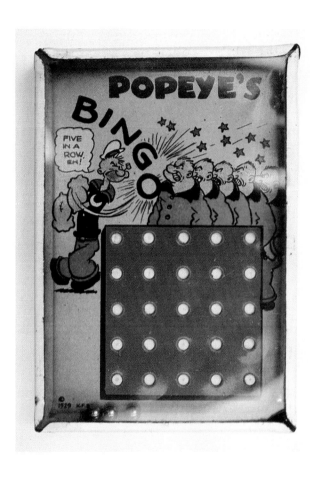

Popeye's Bingo
(King Features Syndicate)
[Bar-Zim Toy Mfg. Co., Inc.]
Metal & Glass
3 1/2" x 5"
$60

Nancy Holding Ice Cream Cone
(United Features Syndicate)
Plastic
2 1/4" Dia.
$25

Sluggo Dancing
(United Features Syndicate)
Plastic
2 1/4" Dia.
$25

Blondie's Ring Toss
(King Features Syndicate)
Tin, Glass, & Cardboard
5" x 3 1/2"
$85

Goofy
(Walt Disney Prod.)
[Made in Hong Kong]
Plastic
2 1/4" Dia.
$35

Donald Duck
(Walt Disney Prod.)
[Made in Germany, 1991]
Aluminum & Plastic
(Mirror on Back)
$10

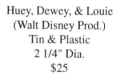

Huey, Dewey, & Louie
(Walt Disney Prod.)
Tin & Plastic
2 1/4" Dia.
$25

Pluto
(Walt Disney Prod.)
Plastic
3" Dia.
$25

Mickey Mouse
(Walt Disney Prod.)
Plastic & Paper
1 5/16" Dia.
$75

Clown Puzzles

Juggling Clown
Cardboard & Plastic
3" Dia.
$30

Clown Looking Above
Tin, Glass & Cardboard (with Mirror on Back)
1 3/4" Dia.
$55

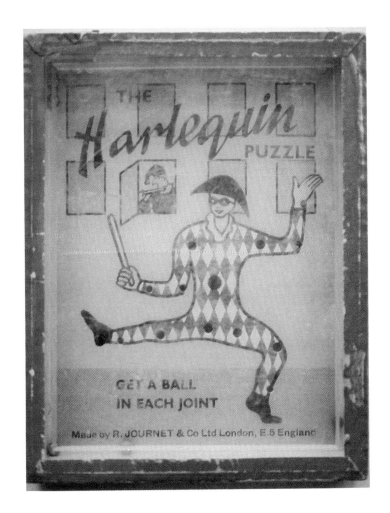

The Harlequin Puzzle
[R. Journet & Co.]
Plastic
4 1/4" x 5 1/4"
$45

Jester
Tin, Glass, & Cardboard
1 3/4" Dia.
$55

Toothless Clown
Cardboard & Plastic
3" Dia.
$25

Clown Ringmaster
[Made in Germany]
Metal & Glass
2 1/4" Dia.
$50

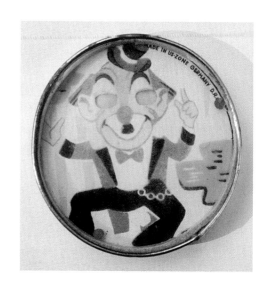

Jolo the Juggling Clown
[A+A American Metal Toy Co.]
Metal & Plastic
5 1/4" x 3 1/2"
$35

Cross-Eyed Clown
Plastic & Cardboard
1" Dia.
$5

Cowboy & Indian Puzzles

Fighting Blue Devils - 101st Cavalry
[Nabisco Shredded Wheat Juniors]
Tin & Plastic
1 1/4" Dia.
$35

Army Wagon
[Nabisco Shredded Wheat Juniors]
Tin & Plastic
1 1/4" Dia.
$30

Pitch'Em Cowboy Puzzle Display
[Plas-Trix Co.]
Games- Plastic   Display- Cardboard
Games- 1 1/2" x 3"
$10 each
Display- 5 3/4" x 10 1/2"
$75

Stagecoach Attack
[Hale-Nass Corp.]
Metal & Plastic
5 1/4" x 3 1/2"
$40

Hopalong Cassidy with Lariat
(Reproduction)
Plastic
2" Dia.
$10

Hopalong Cassidy Draw!
(Reproduction)
Plastic
2" Dia.
$10

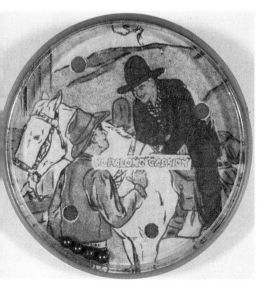

Hopalong Cassidy with Lucky
(Reproduction)
Plastic
2" Dia.
$10

Lone Ranger Series #1
[T.L.R., Inc.]
Tin, Glass, & Cardboard
5" x 3 1/2"
$60

Lone Ranger Series #3
[T.L.R., Inc.]
Tin, Glass, & Cardboard
5" x 3 1/2"
$60

(Above) Lone Ranger Series #2
[T.L.R., Inc.]
Tin, Glass, & Cardboard
5" x 3 1/2"
$60

(Below) Lone Ranger Series #4
[T.L.R., Inc.]
Tin, Glass, & Cardboard
5" x 3 1/2"
$60

Colorful Cowboy with Both Guns Drawn
[Made in Hong Kong]
Plastic
2" Dia.   1950
$20

Following Page (Upper Photo)
Bank Robbery
[A+A American Metal Toy Co.]
Metal & Plastic
5 1/4" x 3 1/2"
$45

Following Page (Lower Photo)
Indians with Captive
[A&A American Metal Toy Co.]
Tin & Plastic
5 1/4" x 3 1/2"
$40

(Above) See Previous Page

(Below) See Previous Page

Cavalry Sergeant with Pistol
[Nabisco Shredded Wheat Juniors]
Tin & Plastic
1 1/4" Dia.
$30

Indian Chief with Beaded Necklace
(Made in Germany)
Metal & Glass
1 1/4" Dia.
$50

101st Cavalry Trooper
[Nabisco Shredded Wheat Juniors]
Tin & Plastic
1 1/4" Dia.
$35

The Covered Wagon
[Made in U.S.A.]
Tin, Glass, & Cardboard
5" x 3 1/2"
$40

Cowboy with Red Pistols & Hat
Cardboard & Plastic
1 1/4" Dia.
$5

Geronimo
[Nabisco Shredded Wheat Juniors]
Tin & Plastic
1 1/4" Dia.
$20

Space Adventure Puzzles

Outer Space City
[Hale- Nass Corporation]
Tin & Plastic
3 1/2" x 5 1/4"
$70

Satellite "Jiggle" Puzzle
[Comon Tatar, Inc.]
Cardboard & Plastic
2 1/2" x 3"   1957
$40

Spaceship Blast-Off
Cardboard & Plastic
2 1/4" Dia.
$55

Spaceship to the Moon
[Baby World - NYC]
2 1/2" Dia.
$30

Spaceman & Rainbow
(Made in Japan)
Cardboard & Plastic
1 7/8" Dia.
$20

Sports Puzzles

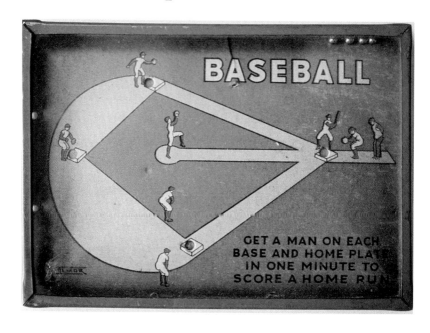

Baseball
Tin & Glass
3 1/2" x 5"
$45

Soccer Player
Plastic & Paper
15/16" Dia.
$20

Golf "Jiggle" Puzzle
[Comon Tatar, Inc.]
Plastic & Cardboard
2 7/16" x 3 1/8"   1957
$30

Homerun King (Pinball-Style)
[Made in Japan]
Wood & Glass
2 1/4" x 4 1/2"
$35

Shotput
Chrome Metal & Glass
1 1/2" Dia.
$25

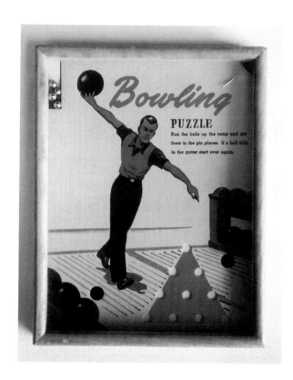

Bowling Puzzle
[Joseph W. Drueke Co.]
Wood, Paper, & Glass
4 1/4" x 5 1/4"   1948
$45

Fishing Skill Game
[Made in Germany]
Glass, Tin, & Paper
3 7/8" Dia.
$35

Double- Sided Soccer Game
(Both Sides Identical)
[Made in Germany]
Glass & Aluminum
2 1/4" Dia.
$45

Bases Full
Tin, Cardboard, & Glass
3 1/2" x 5"
$35

Horseshoe Puzzle
Tin, Glass, & Cardboard
2 1/2" x 3 1/2"
$40

Badminton Game
[Made in Germany]
Metal & Glass
(Mirror on Back)
1 1/4" Dia.
$35

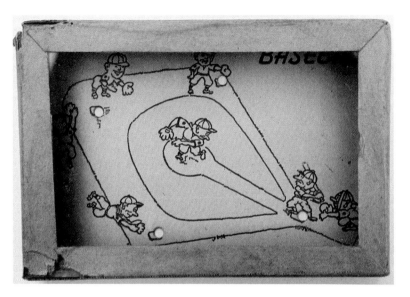

Baseball Puzzle
Cardboard & Glass
3 1/4" x 5"
$40

Basketball Puzzle
[Made in Germany]
Metal & Glass
4" Dia.
$45

Foxhunt Puzzle
[R. Journet & Co.]
Wood & Glass
3 1/4" x 4 1/4"
$50

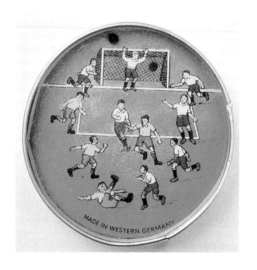

Scrambling Soccer Teams
[Made in Germany]
Metal & Glass
(Mirror on Back)
2 1/4" Dia.
$30

Foxhunt Puzzle (Variation)
[R. Journet & Co.]
[Remanufactured by Wm. F. Drueke & Sons, Inc.]
Plastic
5 1/4" x 4 1/8"
$35

Scrambling Soccer Team (Variation)
[Made in Germany]
Aluminum & Plastic
(Mirror on Back)
2 1/4" Dia.
$30

Children's Game of Ring Toss
[Colmor]
Tin, Glass, & Cardboard
3 1/2" x 5"
$50

Soccer Puzzle
[Made in Germany]
Tin & Glass
(Mirror on Back)
2 1/4" Dia.
$30

War Related Puzzles

Keep 'Em Rolling For Victory
[Made in U.S.A.]
Tin, Glass, & Cardboard
$75

Paris Battle Scene
Tin & Glass
2 1/2" Dia.
$125

Cootie Game
Tin, Cardboard, & Glass
4" x 5"
$50

Trap A Sap
Tin, Glass, & Cardboard
3 1/4" x 4 1/4"
$50

Following Page (Upper Photo)
Blackout
[Made in U.S.A.]
Tin, Glass, & Cardboard
$45

Following Page (Lower Photo)
Atomic Bomb
[A.C. Gilbert Co.]
Cardboard & Glass
3 1/2" x 4 1/4"   ca. 1948
$65

(Above) See Previous Page   (Below) See Previous Page

Dive-Bomber
Cardboard & Glass
5" x 3 1/4"
$40

Buy U.S. War Bonds and Stamps
Cardboard & Plastic
3 1/2" x 3 1/2"
$85

Bead Games With Rectangular Frames

Hi Score
[Cracker Jack Co.]
Fibered Paper & Plastic
1" x 1 1/2"
$10

Fortune Teller
[Cracker Jack Co.]
Plastic
1" x 1 3/4"
$10

Road Runner
[Cracker Jack Co.]
Plastic & Cardboard
1" x 1 1/2"
$10

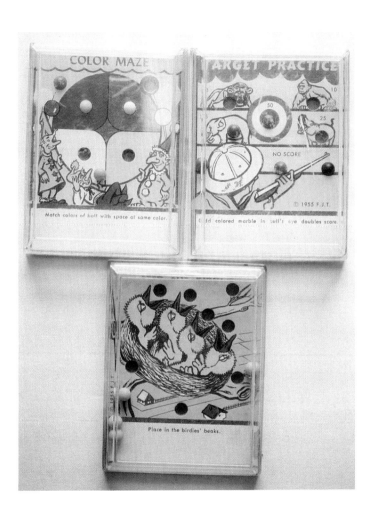

Plastic Hand Held Games
[F.J.T.]
1 1/2" x 3"   1955
Color Maze: $20
Target Practice: $20
Feed the Birds: $20

The Diver's Puzzle
[R. Journet & Co.]
Wood & Glass
4 1/4" x 5"
$30

Great Snakes
[Made in Germany]
Glass & Cardboard
2 5/8" x 7 1/2"
$60

Striped Cat Puzzle
[Made in Germany]
Wood & Plastic
2 1/4" Square
$15

Spider Puzzle
Tin, Glass, & Cardboard
3 1/2" x 5"
$30

Chinese Dragon Puzzle
[Made in England]
Glass & Cardboard
2 3/4" x 4 1/4"
$30

Ferris Wheel Puzzle
[Columbia Mfg. Co., Baltimore, MD]
Cardboard, Wood, & Glass
5" x 5"   1894
$100

Following Page (Upper Photo)
Station Lunch Room
[Colmor]
Tin, Glass, & Cardboard
5" x 3 1/2"
$30

Following Page (Lower Photo)
Mary, Mary, Quite Contrary
Plastic & Cardboard
2 3/8" x 3 1/8"
$10

(Above) See Previous Page   (Below) See Previous Page

Circus Seals
[Made in U.S.A.]
Tin, Glass, & Cardboard
5" x 3 1/2"
$35

Rabbits in Corn
[R. Journet & Co.]
Plastic
4 1/2" x 5 1/2"
$25

Are You on the Ball?
[Milton Bradley Co.]
Plastic & Cardboard
Box 9 1/2" x 5" x 2 1/2"   1964
$10 $20 with Box

Fill in the Artist's Palette
[Colmor]
Tin, Glass, & Cardboard
5" x 3 1/2"
$35

Three Blind Mice
[Comon Tatar Inc.]
Plastic & Cardboard
3" x 2 1/4"   1960
$25

Bingo!
[Colmor]
Cardboard & Glass
3 1/4" x 5"
$20

Dipsy Ball Puzzle
[Adams Mfg. Co.]
Plastic
2 1/2" x 1"
$10

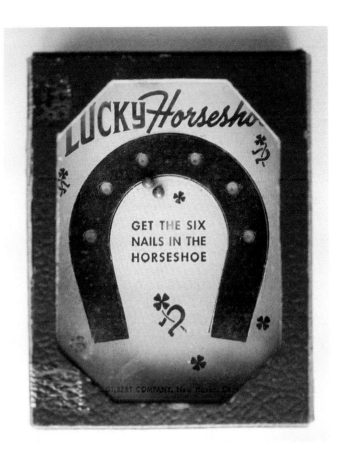

Lucky Horseshoe
[A.C. Gilbert Co.]
Cardboard & Glass
3 1/4" x 4 1/4"
$30

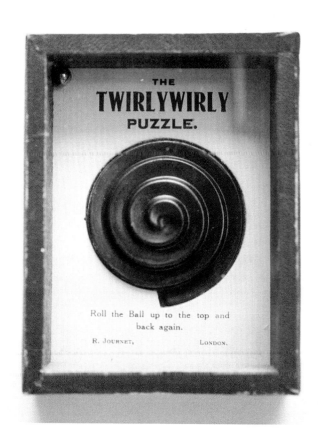

The Twirlywirly Puzzle "with Red Frame"
[R. Journet & Co.]
Wood, Glass, & Cardboard
3 1/4" x 4 1/4"
$40

Twirlywirly Puzzle "with Yellow Frame"
[R. Journet & Co.]
Plastic & Wood
4" x 5"
$40

"Kanuduit" Puzzle
[R. Journet & Co.]
Wood & Glass
3 3/8" x 4 1/4"
$30

Sing A Song of Sixpence
[Comon Tatar, Inc.]
Plastic & Cardboard
3" x 2 1/4"   1960
$25

Frog Puzzle
Tin, Glass, & Cardboard
3 1/2" x 5"
$40

Alice in Wonderland
[J.W. Drueke]
Wood & Glass
4" x 5"   1952
$40

The Dovecote Puzzle
[R. Journet & Co., Ltd.]
Wood & Plastic
5 1/4" x 4 1/8"
$35

Cogwheel Puzzle
Tin, Glass, & Cardboard
3 1/2" x 5"
$40

Pigs in Clover Puzzle
[Wm. F. Drueke & Sons, Inc.]
Plastic & Cardboard
5" x 4"   1950
$25

Bead Games With Round Frames

Two-Sided Dexterity Game
Cardboard & Glass
2" Dia.
$35

Train Puzzle
Aluminum, Glass, & Cardboard
2 1/8" Dia.
$40

Underside of Train Puzzle

Two-Sided Skill Game
[Made in Japan]
Glass & Paper
1 1/4" x 2 3/4" Dia.
$25

Other Side of Game Noted Above

Yellow Mouth Monkey
[Made in Japan]
Plastic
1 7/8" Dia.   1950
$15

Monkey & Stars
[Made in Japan]
Cardboard & Plastic
2" Dia.   1950
$10

Red-Eyed Monkey
[Made in Japan]
Cardboard & Plastic
1 1/2" Dia.   1950
$10

Owl Puzzle
[Made in Japan]
Cardboard & Plastic
1 1/2" Dia.   1950
$10

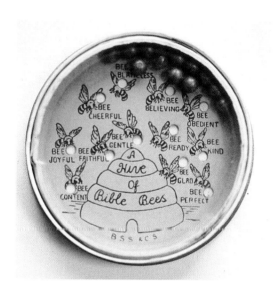

A Hive of Bible Bees
Cardboard & Plastic
2 3/8" Dia.
$40

Butterfly
Glass, Aluminum, & Cardboard
2 1/4" Dia.
$20

Duck in Sailor Suit
[Made in Japan]
Plastic & Cardboard
2 7/8" Dia.
$20

Pelican Feeding Young
[Made in Germany]
Aluminum, Glass, & Cardboard
1 1/2" Dia.
$25

Santa Claus Puzzle
Cardboard & Plastic
2 1/4" Dia.
$20

Following Page (Upper Photo)
Two-Sided Dexterity Game
(Monkey Side)
[Made in Japan]
Cardboard & Glass
$30

Following Page (Lower Photo)
India Dice Game
(Reverse Side of Same Game)

(See Previous Page)

93

Miniature Roulette
[Made in Japan]
Tin & Glass
2 5/8" Dia.
$25

Elephant in Suit
[Made in Germany]
Aluminum, Glass, & Cardboard
1 3/8" Dia.
$40

Men at Water Well
Aluminum,. Glass, & Cardboard
(Mirror on Back)
2 1/8" Dia.
$35

Dogs at Tug-O-War
Aluminum, Glass, & Cardboard
1 7/8" Dia.
$25

Man, Sea Shell, & Swan
Aluminum, Glass, & Cardboard
(Mirror on Back)
2 1/8" Dia.
$35

Jack-in-the-Box
[Made in Germany]
Tin, Glass, & Cardboard
(Mirror on Back)
1 1/8" Dia.
$25

Boys and Hatchling
[Foreign]
Aluminum, Glass, & Cardboard
2 1/4" Dia.
$25

Duck with Clown Hat
[Made in Japan]
Cardboard & Plastic
1 1/2" Dia.   1950
$20

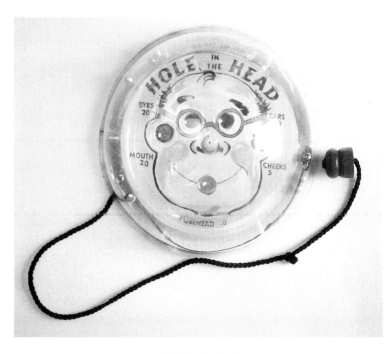

Hole in the Head
[Electric Games Co.]
5" Dia. x 3 1/2"   1946
$25

Peasant in Red Hat
Tin & Glass
1 1/8" Dia.
$45

Rosy Checks
[Made in Japan]
Cardboard & Plastic
2" Dia.
$20

Smiling Baby
[Made in Japan]
Cardboard & Plastic
2" Dia.   1950
$20

The "Coronation" Puzzle
["Tip Top" Series]
Tin & Glass (Mirror on Back)
2 1/2" Dia.
$75

German House
Glass, Aluminum, & Cardboard
(Mirror on Back)
2 1/8" Dia.
$45

Babies in Cradle
[Made in Germany]
Aluminum, Glass, & Cardboard
2 1/8" Dia.
$35

Man and Baby Gator
[Made in Germany]
Aluminum, Glass, & Cardboard
(Mirror on Back)
2 1/4" Dia.
$45

Childrens' Silhouette
[D.R.G. Manufacturing]
Tin & Glass (Mirror on Back)
2 1/4" Dia.
$45

Man with Cap & Cigar
Glass, Paper, & Metal
(Mirror on Back)
1 5/16" Dia.
$25

Little Red Riding Hood
Cardboard & Plastic
2 1/2" Dia.
$25

Rabbits Helping Wolf
[Made in Germany]
2" Dia.
$35

Girl With Umbrella
[Made in Japan]
Cardboard & Glass
2 1/4" Dia.
$15

Bulldog
[Made in Japan]
Cardboard & Plastic
1 1/2" Dia.   1950
$15

Cow Wearing Glasses
[Made in Japan]
Cardboard & Plastic
1 1/2" Dia.   1950
$15

Yellow Fox
[Made in Japan]
Cardboard & Plastic
1 1/2" Dia.   1950
$15

Teddy Bear & Bowtie
[Made in Japan]
Cardboard & Plastic
1 1/2" Dia.   1950
$15

Boxing Kangaroo
Cardboard & Plastic
1 1/8" Dia.
$15

Kangaroo & Baby Kangaroo
Aluminum, Glass, & Cardboard
(Mirror on Back)
2 1/4" Dia.
$35

Panda Bear
Plastic
1 1/4" Dia.
$10

Black Terrier
[Made in Germany]
Metal & Plastic
(Mirror on Back)
2" Dia.
$15

Lion
Plastic
1 1/4" Dia.
$5

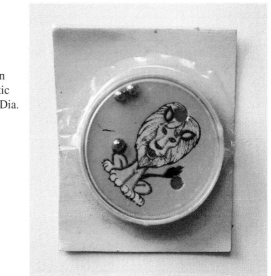

Grazing Cow
Plastic
1 1/4" Dia.
$5

Elephant Puzzle (Two-Sided Puzzle)
[Made in Japan]
Cardboard & Glass
2 3/4" Dia.
$25

(Reverse Side of Elephant Puzzle)

Accordion Player
[Made in Occupied Japan]
Metal & Glass
(Mirror on Back)
2" Dia.
$15

Ladybug
[Made in Germany]
Plastic
1 3/4" Dia.
$15

Bear Juggling Barrel (Two-Sided Puzzle)
[Made in Japan]
Cardboard & Plastic
2 3/4" Dia.
$25

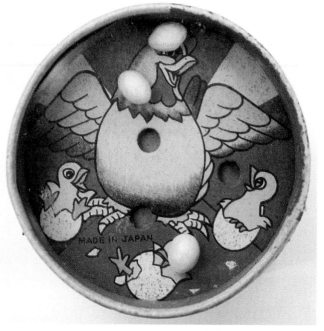

(Reverse Side of
Bear Juggling
Barrel Puzzle)

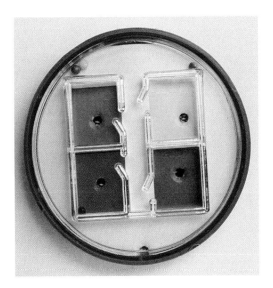

Color Squares Puzzle
Plastic
2 1/2" Dia.
$10

Cable Car Puzzle
[Made in Germany]
Aluminum & Glass
2" Dia.
$15

Squirrel Puzzle
[Made in Japan]
Cardboard & Plastic
2 1/4" Dia.
$10

Old Man in Pajamas
[Made in Germany]
Tin & Glass
2 1/4" Dia.
$30

Worrisome King
[Made in Japan]
2 1/2" Dia.
Cardboard & Glass
$25

Red & Green Ramp Puzzle
[Made in Germany]
Tin & Glass
(Mirror on Back)
2" Dia.
$20

Seven Spoons Puzzle
[Made in Germany]
Tin & Glass
(Mirror on Back)
2" Dia.
$25

Girl & Doll Carriage
Plastic
2 1/4" Dia.
$5

Gnome & Pigeon
Tin & Glass
(Mirror on Back)
2 1/4" Dia.
$35

Red Riding Hood & Wolf
[Made in Germany]
Aluminum & Glass
(Mirror on Back)
2 1/4" Dia.
$30

Kitten
[Made in Japan]
Cardboard & Plastic
1 3/4" Dia.
$15

Gorilla
[Made in Japan]
Cardboard & Plastic
1 1/2" Dia.
$15

Hedgehog Puzzle
[Made in Germany]
Plastic
1 3/4" Dia.
$15

Men Driving Touring Car
[Made in Germany]
Tin & Glass
1 1/4" Dia.
$35

Anitque Auto
[Made in Germany]
Aluminum & Glass
2 1/4" Dia.
$25

Birds on Brick Wall
[Made in Germany]
(A Souvenir from the Universal Theatres
Concession Co., Chicago, IL)
Tin & Glass
(Mirror on Back)
1 1/4" Dia.
$35

Pink Pussycat
[Made in Germany]
Tin & Glass
(Mirror on Back)
2 1/4" Dia.
$25

Dog with Eyes & Eyebrows
[Made in Germany]
Tin & Glass
(Mirror on Back)
2" Dia.
$25

Young Barber
[Made in Germany]
Tin & Glass
(Mirror on Back)
2 1/4" Dia.
$30

Wondering Puppy
[Made in Japan]
Cardboard & Glass
1 3/4" Dia.
$15

Misc. Games With Rectangular Frames

Pin-U-Ringit
[R. Journet & Co.]
Plastic
4 1/2" x 5 1/2"
$15

Ringtail Cat Puzzle
[R. Journet & Co.]
Wood & Glass
4 1/4" x 3 1/4"
$30

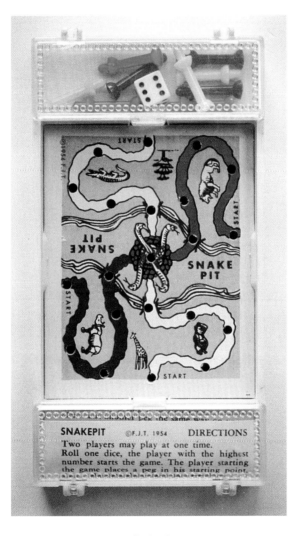

Snakepit
[F.J.T. Co.]
Plastic
3" x 5 1/2"   1954
$20

China Checkers
[F.J.T. Co.]
Plastic
3" x 5 1/4"   1954
$20

The American Way
Tin & Glass
5" x 3 1/2"
$65

The "Golden Rod" Puzzle
[R. Journet & Co.]
Glass & Cardboard
3 1/4" x 4 1/2"
$30

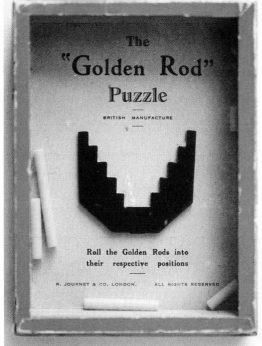

The Merry Toast Puzzle
[R. Journet & Co.]
Wood & Glass
4 1/4" x 5"
$30

Garden of Eden
[Convex Sign Co.]
Tin & Plastic
5 11/16" x 5"   1925
$150

The Piggybak Puzzle
[R. Journet & Co.]
Wood & Plastic
4 1/4" x 5"
$30

The Bughouse
[Bar-Zim Toy Mfg. Co., Inc.]
Metal & Glass
4" x 3 1/2"
$50

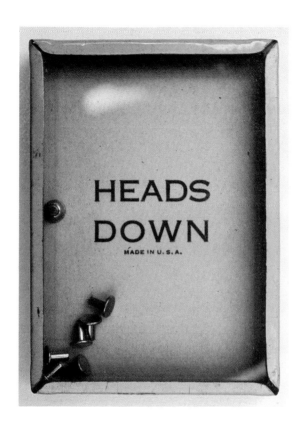

Heads Down
[Made in U.S.A.]
Metal & Glass
3 1/2" x 2 1/2"
$25

Misc. Games With Round Frames

Cat & Mouse
[Made in Occupied Japan]
Plastic & Glass
2 1/8" Dia.
$45

Fishbowl
[The C.J. Co.]
Cardboard & Plastic
1 1/2" Dia.
$10

Cobbler Blowing Smoke Rings
[D.R.G.N.]
Tin & Glass (Mirror on Back)
2 1/4" Dia.
$45

Man Puffing Cigar
[The C.J. Co.]
Plastic & Cardboard
1 1/2" Dia.
$10

"Jitney- Bus Game"
[Allen Bros.]
Brass & Glass
2" Dia.   1916
$65

Dice Game
Tin & Glass
1 1/4" Dia.
$20

Shake-A-Face Puzzle
[Made in Germany]
Cardboard & Plastic
2 3/8" Dia.
$20

Shake-A-Face Puzzle
[Made in Germany]
Metal & Glass
1 3/4" Dia.
$30

Shake A Face Puzzle
[Made in Germany]
Aluminum, Plastic, & Cardboard
2 1/4" Dia.
$30

Bird on Branch
[The C.J. Co.]
Cardboard & Plastic
1 1/2" Dia.
$10

Shake-A-Face Puzzle
[Made in Germany]
Plastic
2 1/4" Dia.
$20

Camel Ring Game
[Made in Japan]
Paper & Glass
1 1/2" x 3 1/2" Dia.
$35

Hanging China Man
Aluminum, Glass, &
Cardboard
(Mirror on Back)
2 1/2" Dia.
$100

Kittens Toying with Mice
[Made in Germany]
Aluminum & Plastic
(Mirror on Back)
2 1/4" Dia.
$40

Cats and Ball
Aluminum, Glass, & Cardboard
(Mirror on Back)
2" Dia.
$25

Adam's Fantom Puzzler - Horse Shoes
Tin, Plastic, & Cardboard
3 1/2" Dia.
$40

Trained Poodles
[Made in Germany]
(A Souvenir from the Universal
Theatres Concession Co., Chicago, IL)
Tin & Glass
(Mirror on Back)
$75

Adam's Bed Bug Puzzle
Tin, Glass, & Cardboard
3 1/2" Dia.
$50

Woman's Portrait
[Made in Germany]
Tin & Glass (Mirror on Back)
1 1/4" Dia.
$50

Who Catches Us?
[D.R.G.M.]
Tin, Glass, & Cardboard
3 7/8" Dia.
$45

Lizard Goes in its Home
[Made in Germany]
Metal & Glass
(Mirror on Back)
2 1/4" Dia.
$75

Ring Monkey's Tail
[Made in Hong Kong]
Plastic
2 1/2" Dia.
$25

(Reverse Side of
Ring Monkey's Tail
Puzzle)

Three Blind Mice
[Made in Japan]
Cardboard & Glass
4" Dia.
$30

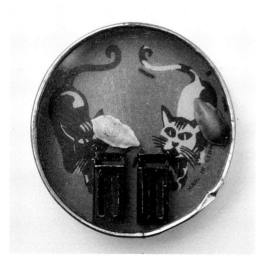

Save Black & White Mice
[Made in Germany]
Tin & Glass
(Mirror on Back)
2" Dia.
$40

Place Rider on Horse Puzzle
[Made in Germany]
Tin & Glass
[Mirror on Back]
2 1/4" Dia.
$50

Make Dog Bite Seat of Boy's Pants Puzzle
[Made in Germany]
Tin & Glass
(Mirror on Back)
2" Dia.
$50

Miss Toy (Two-Sided Puzzle)
[Made in Japan]
Cardboard & Glass
2 3/4" Dia.
$40

(Reverse side of Miss Toy Puzzle)

Rabbit & Bear
[Made in Japan]
Glass & Cardboard
2 3/4" Dia.
$35

(Reverse Side of Rabbit & Bear Puzzle)

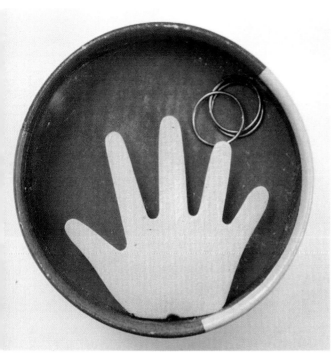

Ring the Fingers
[Made in Japan]
Cardboard &
Glass
2 3/4" Dia.
$30

(Reverse Side of Ring the Fingers Puzzle)

MADE IN JAPAN

Cat and Mouse Game
[Common Tatar Inc.]
Plastic
7 3/4" Dia.   1966
$15

Three Blind Mice Magic Illusion Game
Metal, Glass, & Plastic
2 1/8" Dia.
$50

El Torero Magic Illusion Game
[Made in U.S.A.]
Metal & Plastic
2 1/4" Dia.
$60

Indu Magic Illusion Game
[Made in Germany]
Tin & Plastic
2 1/8" Dia.
$80

Puzzle Sets

Gilbert Boxed Problem Puzzles
[A.C. Gilbert Co.]
Cardboard & Glass
Box - 10 3/8" x 8 7/8"   1940
$275

(See Following Page)

Gilbert Boxed Problem Puzzles
(Contains the Following:)

Ball and Gear
Ring A Tail
Hungry Pup
Ring A Peg
Radio Tube Trick
Topsy Turvy Rivets
$40 each

The Jeep Board - 15 Games & 10 Puzzles
(Designed Exclusively for Men in the US Armed Forces)
[George S. Carrington Co.]
Wood & Glass (with twine to strap to leg)
Box - 3 1/2" x 3 3/4"   1943
$60

Puzzle Box
[Abercrombie & Fitch Co.]
Box - 9" x 4 3/4" x 6 1/2"
(Holds Eleven Dexterity Games)

(Enclosed games priced on following eleven pages)

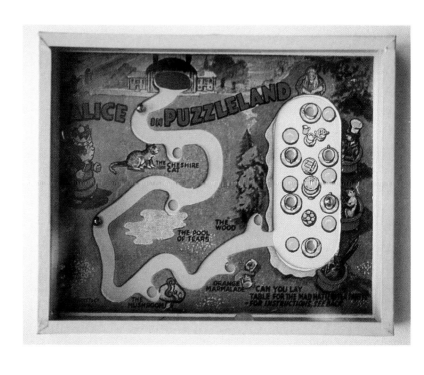

Alice in Puzzleland
[R. Journet & Co.]
Wood & Glass
4 1/4" x 5"
$45
(Available in Abercrombie Puzzle Box or Separately)
(See Page 149)

The Cog Wheel Puzzle
[R. Journet & Co.]
Wood & Plastic
4 1/4" x 5"
$40

(Available in Abercrombie Puzzle Box or Separately)
(See Page 149)

The "Queen Mary" Puzzle
[R. Journet & Co.]
Plastic
5 1/4" x 4"
$50

(Available in Abercrombie Puzzle Box or Separately)
(See Page 149)

The "Pondsnag" Puzzle
[R. Journet & Co.]
Wood & Glass
4 1/4" x 5"
$45

(Available in Abercrombie Puzzle Box or Separately)
(See Page 149)

The Double-Six Puzzle
[R. Journet & Co.]
Wood & Glass
4 1/4" x 5"
$35

(Available in Abercrombie Puzzle Box or Separately)
(See Page 149)

The Turnstile Puzzle
[R. Journet & Co.]
Wood & Glass
4 1/4" x 5"
$30

(Available in Abercrombie Puzzle Box or Separately)
(See Page 149)

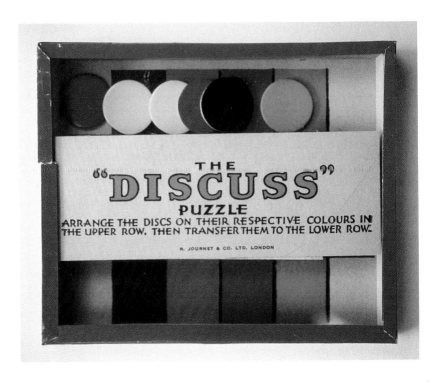

The "Discuss" Puzzle
[R. Journet & Co.]
Wood & Glass
4 1/4" x 5"
$35

(Available in Abercrombie Puzzle Box or Separately)
(See Page 149)

Aero Puzzle
[R. Journet & Co.]
Wood & Glass
4 1/4" x 5"
$45

(Available in Abercrombie Puzzle Box or Separately)
(See Page 149)

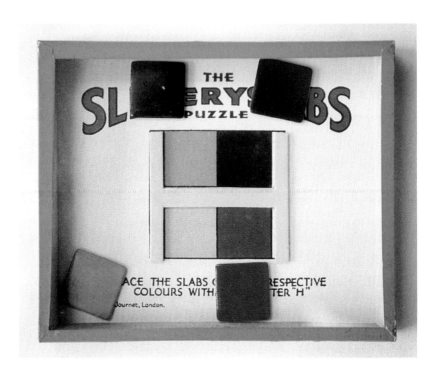

The Slipperyslabs Puzzle
[R. Journet & Co.]
Wood & Glass
4 1/4" x 5"
$30

(Available in Abercrombie Puzzle Box or Separately)
(See Page 149)

The Lucky Seven Domino Puzzle
[R. Journet & Co.]
Wood & Glass
$ 1/4" x 5"
$35

(Available in Abercrombie Puzzle Box or Separately)
(See Page 149)

790.1
DEX

Collector's digest
dexterity games and other
hand-held puzzles.

ELK

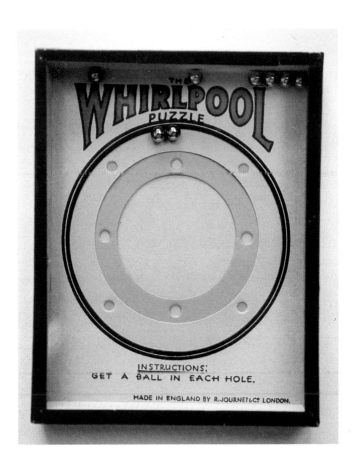

The Whirlpool Puzzle
[R. Journet & Co.]
Wood & Glass
4 1/4" x 5"
$30

(Available in Abercrombie Puzzle Box or Separately)
(See Page 149)